Reviews

"I know the many precautions and hidden dangers when investigating the paranormal due to Peter James' work, knowing my own personal experiences in a former active haunted residence, and attending dozens of documented team paranormal investigations. Though, and as you will learn, many more dangers can potentially reveal themselves when dealing with the unknown. With what is 'paranormal', 'normal' never usually applies, and ANYTHING is possible; as this team of paranormal researches will soon find out…"

Gian Temperilli – Is the co-author and editor of "Heaven Can You Hear Me?" by late famed FOX "Sightings" televised psychic and legendary paranormal researcher, Peter James. Gian currently co-hosts his daughter's wildly popular weekly broadcast on LiveParanormal.com, "The Ghost Host" with Sophia Temperilli…

~~~

Reviews

Other books available

*Paratales- Paranormal Short stories
*So You Want To Be a Ghost Hunter

More to come….

Ghost Hunted
The beginning of the Mike Taylor series

By Jason Hess

Edited by
Kanda Delisle

DragonEye Publishing

Ghost Hunted
The beginning of the Mike Taylor series
By Jason Hess
Copyright 2013 by Jason Hess

All rights reserved. No part of this book may be reproduced by any means or in any form whatsoever without written permission from the Author and Publisher, except for brief quotation embodied in literary articles or reviews.

Edited by Kanda Delisle

First Edition
First Printing – June 2013

ISBN 13: 978-1-61500-042-5 (Trade Paperback)
ISBN 13: 978-1-61500-069-8 (EPub Ebook)
ISBN 13: 978-1-61500-164-4 (PDF)

Library of Congress Control Number: 2013902982

Visit our website
wwwDragonEyePublishers.com

Published by DragonEye Publishing

DragonEye Publishing
753 Linden Place, Unit A
Elmira, NY 14901

Dedicated to Sonya Harris
A mother, a fighter, and a friend
R.I.P.

1

They say everything has a purpose, as such, so should everyone. Right now it's eight in the morning and I am only on my first cup of coffee. In other words, I am not awake and I am getting bitched at, yet again.

My name is Mike Taylor and I am getting yelled at by my girlfriend. Her name is Samantha Simmons and she's running late for work. She is a nurse and works for a high profile doctor downtown. I got lucky when I met her; she's five foot ten and has an athletic body. She has the face of an angel, and brains to match. What a woman!

Me, well I am an average guy and I have a degree in Business Management.

Ghost Hunted

Unfortunately, I am unemployed. I got laid off from the car lot I was selling used cars at. That was six months ago. I have been living off a trust fund left to me when my Grandfather passed away. And that is starting to run out. I really need a new job!

The thing that bothers Samantha is the last interview I was on was 2 months ago. Hey, I have a lot going on in my life! There's um…..and I've got……well there's the group. See I am the founder of V.G.H. That stands for Virginia Ghost Hunters. Yes I am a Paranormal Investigator, or otherwise known as a ghost hunter. No it's not like in the movies where they run in with proton packs and traps, this is real.

"So you better be going out looking for a job today. All you have been doing is sitting around the house screwing around on the computer!" said Samantha.

"I have been working, and I have been looking for work. Anyways, Todd called me and told me that the dealer was going to start calling people back this week."

"You know if you paid the same attention to me as you do to your computer maybe I wouldn't be so lonely in bed at night. Also going over group things isn't work, it's a hobby. You don't get paid and you keep buying stuff for hunts." she replied. "I am in the group too, but there is more to life than just ghosts. You're the only person I know that spends his whole day doing this. It's got to change and it's got to change now!"

"Honey, I…"

"Don't. Don't even try to explain! I am late for work and I have to go make money for us. You better have a job by next week. I don't even care if you're flipping burgers. End of story!" Samantha said angrily as she put her shoes on. "I mean it Mike, or you're out of here! I cannot keep supporting both of us."

She stood up and stared at me for a second then turned and walked away, grabbed her purse and walked out the door. And she didn't even say good bye! I thought that was kind of rude. And how can I be out of here? It's my damn house, and it's paid for. I think it's best to just let her cool down and all will be good tonight.

See, we live in a little Cape Cod house on the outskirts of Richmond, Virginia. It's not a huge plantation; it's just a suburban home on a suburban block in the suburbs. It has two bedrooms downstairs, a kitchen, and living room. Upstairs is my office for the group. That's where I spend most of my time.

So I walk into the kitchen to get a refill of coffee and notice that it is a beautiful fall day; the leaves are just starting to change. And it's starting to come into the group's busy season. For some reason everyone and their brother thinks their house is haunted, I guess there are too many scary movies on TV.

I walked out of the kitchen and started to head upstairs and heard a loud groan. This would be my dog, the laziest dog in the world. Three years ago I fell in love with a playful basset hound pup, and if he didn't groan once in a while you would think that he is a statue. We named him Ralph because the dog ate everything then in turn puked it all up. Ok, there is nothing is better than a regurgitated battery!

I stopped to pet Ralph and continued upstairs. Off to my space, with all my gadgets to fuel my passion! Yes it's a passion I have had ever since I was a kid.

When I was ten I saw my first ghost. It happened while we were on a nice family vacation to Gettysburg. It didn't happen on the battlefield like people would think. It was in the museum.

We were looking at some uniforms and guns which I thought were cool at the time. And I swear I saw a man's face in the glass of the display. I looked behind me and no one was there. So I turned back towards the display and it was gone from there too. I ran back to my parents and told them what I saw, and they thought it was just my imagination.

That was the beginning of my interest with the afterlife. Some questions are why they haven't moved on and how they exist? All these years later and I still don't know.

So on to my normal routine, sit in front of the computer and network. That consists of checking my emails and hit all the social network sites. I might hit a few games on there, oh yea and look for a job too.

I still have audio to go over from our last case. It was a waste of time, but we have to be sure there isn't anything there. So far it has been as quiet as an empty library.

Just about that time the phone rang, which I forgot downstairs, so back down stairs I go.

I got down the stairs and ran to the phone; just as I got it in my hand it stopped ringing. Figures! It's just like when you are getting quality reading time in the bathroom!

So with phone in hand I went back upstairs. Halfway up the stairs the phone rang again. This time I picked it up on the first ring.

"Hello." I said

I just heard heavy breathing in the background and then a scratchy soft voice.

"I want to hire you." said the voice.

I could tell it was a woman, and she sounded old. I didn't apply anywhere that had really old people.

"Excuse me?"

"I want to hire you. A ghost killed my husband."

Ok now my interest is peaked. For one, they want an investigation, and two she just said a ghost killed her husband. Highly unlikely but we will see.

"Ok I believe you just said a ghost killed your husband. Can you tell me more?"

"32 Farm Lane. Come tonight. I'll pay you five thousand dollars." she said. "Be there at seven and start. I will be there some time later, it's unlocked."

With every word she said I thought that she was going to die right there on the phone. The gasping for air and the voice, I guess she has been a heavy smoker for a century or so.

"Can I get your name ma'am? Then I can schedule..."

"Seven." and she disconnected.

Ok this is a little weird but wow five grand to go to the old bitty's house and find out the lead paint killed her husband! I guess it's time to text the team about tonight! Samantha is going to kill me.

After sending a mass text to everyone, confirmations start coming back in. There are only six members in the group including Sam and I.

Tammy is an IT specialist and killer with computers. She works at an insurance company and is an IT trouble shooter. Tammy created and maintains our website plus has developed an editing program so we can analyze our audio.

Our camera man is Kevin, and he has been with the group since the beginning. He has a degree in Chemistry but actually cleans up dog crap at a pet store. Why, I don't even know.

Carrie and Mark are married with children. Mark and I grew up together and were on that vacation to Gettysburg. So we have had the same interest since a young age.

Now his wife is our group's sensitive, a psychic medium to most people. She can see and hear things most of us can't. We can't use what she says as proof, but she brings them out so we may capture audio or visual evidence of the occurrence.

Audio evidence we capture is called EVPS, electronic voice phenomenon. I have over a thousand different disembodied voices picked up over the years. The best we have captured was the sound of two women talking. There are two distinct voices and they are carrying on a conversation.

Now that the team is all set to go I have to get them to the house before Samantha gets home and starts complaining about how tired she is and how she is not going to go. As long as the group is already here she will feel like she has no choice but to go. This also will keep her from yelling at me, hopefully.

I have to get all the cameras charging and everything all packed up. We have a few voice recorders and headphones, as well as video cameras with infrared night vision. Also, we have a security system with the same type of lenses.

We use all sorts of different tools, such as a trifield meter to measure the electromagnetic field in an area. It's said that when a spirit tries to manifest itself it creates an energy field.

We also take temperature readings to check for cold spots. To create an energy field a spirit can use heat as energy and be able to show themselves. Now in a demonic haunt we may also find a warm spot, we still haven't come upon this and deep down inside, I really wish we would!

Dozens of batteries and note pads, laptop, umm... I think its all set. Just have to wait for the cams to charge and get them packed. Cases, bags, and reels of drop cords, I am very glad I have a van to put all this in.

Now I have to try and find some information about this house. Just do a search on the address; well maybe use several different search engines. Nothing at all, what the hell. You can find everything on the web but I just can't find out anything on this property.

This might take a while, well no job hunting today. We are going after ghosts!

2

After searching for most of the day I still have found nothing about the property. I really don't like going into a house we really don't know anything about. But for five grand, I'll go.

The team will be here in a half hour and Sam will be home shortly after that. She hates weekday investigations, mainly because she has to go to work in the morning. There were times I went to work without sleep, unfortunately not lately.

So since they will be here soon, I guess I will start loading the van. I got this old cargo van a few years back just for investigations. It's just this side of a piece of crap; no it's just a piece of crap but it serves its purpose quite well.

It's around five to five and Tammy is the first to get here. So I filled her in as much as I could, since there wasn't much to go off of it didn't take long.

Shortly after Tammy arrived, Carrie and Mark pulled up to the house. Of course Carrie brought her bag of tricks.

Things in her bag wouldn't be called scientific but helps her to lead us to active areas. I personally don't believe in all this crystal and salt crap, but it works for her and helps us.

So as we all stand around the van, Samantha pulls into the drive.

"Mike what is going on, don't tell me someone called! I'm not going; I had a terrible day…." Samantha started. "All I want to do is to jump in a hot bath with a bottle of wine."

"Sam, we got a case and they want to pay us a lot of money to do this."

"Mike can we talk?" said Samantha.

As we walked to the door I explained what I knew and how much money it is. I could give her my share for the bills and everything. It might just buy me some time on finding a job.

See we never charge anyone; we do every investigation for free. And every time we go out, it cost us money.

She finally agreed to go and went into the bedroom to change. I proceeded to walk out and join the rest of the group out by the van.

"Well, all we need now is Kevin." I stated.

Kevin is in his own world and runs on Kevin time. That's why I think he is working at the pet store. There's always time to shovel crap. If he wasn't such a great camera man I would probably tell him to just stay home.

I don't know how but he knows where we are going before anyone says anything.

Samantha came out the front door throwing her purse over her shoulder, I knew that look. That look tells me "Mother Nature" called and I won't be getting any loving for a while.

"Why do you schedule these things when I have my…."

"Like I plan when I get the call." I interrupted Sam. "She called me, not the other way around."

Like I keep track of her period and set up a hunt on that day. I should keep track, maybe, but if she is late she tells me right away.

"Mike let's just call Kevin and get on our way! We are burning time and to tell you the truth I want to get this over with!"

Mark was always the one to push for time. He is a human clock and gets bored easy. This one time we were in an abandoned cemetery and I needed to go into the woods.

I told him I would be back in a couple of minutes and he called out every minute that I was gone. Can you say annoying?

At that moment the silent neighborhood was disturbed. The sound of eighties hair band music blasted through the streets, all coming from an old Ford from the same era. Yes, Kevin was making his grand entrance!

Well now that we are all together we could go over a general game plan. That is if Kevin can get his ass out of the car, damn he is playing pretend drums on his steering wheel again!

When the song ended he shut off his car and then the silence was back. Until the creaking of his car door then the sudden slam, then another slam, he finally got it closed on the third try. But as he did a half a pound of rust fell off his quarter panel, but he didn't care. He just walked right up to us and with all his wisdom he said "Hey!"

See Kevin is a little different than the rest of us; we all grew up after college. He is stuck in the partying stage and never got out of it, but when it comes to the hunt he is all business.

Today he is in jean shorts an old concert t-shirt, and an old baseball cap. It's the same cap on every investigation. The bad thing is it stinks from years of sweat and grime.

Tammy at one time had a small crush on him until he came to a meeting smelling like a kennel and had dog crap stuck to his shoe. So she then said" "I think not." Since then she has had a few boyfriends but nothing serious.

"Ok guys, first thanks because of the short notice, but we have a hot case. Plus for the first time in the groups' history they are going to pay us!" I continued to explain what I knew, but the news of getting money was shocking to everyone. See we provide a service, and never ask for anything in return.

"So we are going in blind?" asked Mark. "This just doesn't seem right. We don't even know the house or what it looks like."

"Dude we go in set up the cams, walk around and collect cash. How hard can that be?" blurted Kevin. "The old lady said she would be there so we are cool!"

To help get this on the way I had to explain a little about what I didn't find out about the house. Yes I had to lie, it wouldn't be the first time I did this to get the group in a building.

"She needs help and I believe we can do that for her. Whether we find something or not we can give this lady closure on her husband's death."

Finally, everyone agreed and we jumped in the cars. Once again Kevin was pissed because no one would let him take his car. I mean how professional would it seem with him rocking out as he pulled up to the client's house.

So I started up the van with Samantha sitting next to me and plugged the address into the GPS and we were off and ready.

3

As we drove it was pretty silent in the van with Sam and me. She knew that I wasn't out looking for a job during the day and she knew I was probably upstairs all day. So what I knew is that I was in some deep doo doo when we got home.

At least it was a short drive and within thirty minutes we were pulling up in front of the house. And what a house it was! It was at least a hundred years old and bigger then all of our houses put together.

I have lived out here all my life and seen many Victorian houses but this one put them all to shame! Well it would if it had been kept up, it needed new paint and the lawn needed to be mowed. The bushes needed a good trim, but you could look past all of that and you could see the hidden beauty.

"Ok Mike, we are here and it looks spooky but I am still a little nervous about us going in." Then Mark took out a cigarette and lit it. "I just don't want to get in trouble for trespassing"

"Look she said that it was unlocked and we could go in. She will be here later and we could have her sign the papers then."

"You don't even have the papers signed! Bro, we can't go in until they are. I am not going to get busted because you got a prank phone call and you fell for it."

"It's not a prank, just trust me." I then had to calm Mark down. See a long time ago I talked him into doing something that got us both an overnight stay in jail. Since then it's hard to get him to go along with anything unless he was sure that nothing was going to happen.

"Ok I will walk up to the door and knock. If no one answers I will then see if it's unlocked like the lady said. If it's locked we turn around and go home." I said. "Any problem with that?"

No one answered so I started up the walk. As I got closer to the house you could really see the neglect. Paint was flaking off the sides and it looks like there was a creature living inside the rotted fascia. It had one of those wrap around porches and I bet at one time old men were telling war stories while drinking lemonade rocking away in rocking chairs.

As I came up to the door I swear I saw someone moving inside the house. I knocked and waited. I knocked again and called out my name to announce I was here. Maybe she got there before us and was scared that we were robbers or something.

After waiting a couple minutes I reached for the door knob and slowly turned it. It was unlocked like the woman said it would be and I opened the door.

"Hello." I called out, "Anyone here? I am Mike from V.G.H and someone called us."

I walked into the foyer and started to look around. It was dark and a musty odor filled my nose. The hard wood floors creaked as I took a step. It didn't look like anyone has been in the house for years.

Over to the right was a table that had a rather clean piece of paper laid on top. It seemed out of place since the rest of the house looked like a dust bunny family moved in. So I picked it up and started to read it.

"Please help me. You have my full permission to go through the house and find the ghost that killed my husband. I will be there soon."

Mrs. Chatterley

Well we have permission, and I guess we now know her name. She probably had to go out to get smokes or an oxygen tank. The voice kept running through my head, the rough winded sound still made me wonder.

At that time a bang echoed through the house. It startled me and I started to walk further in the house to see where the noise came from. I walked into what looked to be a parlor and saw a light switch. I reached to switch it on and the light bulb blew in the lamp next to me.

"Well?" said a voice behind me.

I must have jumped about three feet in the air before I realized the voice was from Carrie! She always seemed to be there when I started to feel like I was about ready to turn tail and run. She is my rock and keeps me strong.

"I found a note from the old lady giving us permission. Plus the house has power so we can start setting up everything."

"Good but I want to walk around first, I feel there are a few spirits here and one isn't too friendly. I think we should walk through first Mike." said Carrie. "Just so we know where to look."

I agreed and reached in my pocket and pulled out my cell phone and called Samantha to tell her what we were doing.

After I disconnected, Carrie and I started to look around and map out the house. We went into the parlor further and looked around. There was a fireplace on the long wall with two stained glass windows on either side. Above the mantel was an old painting of a man and woman.

"I wonder if that's Mrs. Chatterley and her husband."

Carrie looked long and hard at the picture and had a very worried look to her. I never liked it when she got this look on her face because it usually meant that something bad was going to happen to me.

"That is her husband but I don't think that is her. The woman in the painting looks to be around twenty years younger than him. And look at the frame, it's been repaired."

She went to touch the frame and as she got close to it Kevin walked in. He was carrying two equipment bags and set them on a couch by the door.

"Since you two are checking out the house I figured we could start bringing in everything and we could get cameras mounted." he said. "And by the time you all get done, we will be ready to set them in place."

We agreed and went out the other door of the room. I pulled out my flashlight and looked around for a light switch. We were in the dining room and there was a table that was at least twelve feet long. And a huge chandelier hung over the table. When the flashlight beam hit the crystals it made a prism effect throughout the room.

Carrie found the switch and flicked it on. Nothing happened. So maybe there was another switch and that one did not work. We continued to walk through the room and the lights went on.

Ok that was a little weird since she was a few feet away from the switch and it went on. I can't wait till we run the emf meter through here!

I looked around and saw all the beautiful mahogany trim and wood panels that lined the room. The table looked like it was the same wood to match. On the left there was a side board and on the right another fireplace.

The lights going on still kind of freaked me out but we had to move on. We passed through the kitchen into a hallway. On the other end of the hallway was the entrance where the team was still bringing in the equipment.

Across from the parlor were the stairs and a doorway that led into a library. Thousands of books filled the built in shelves that lined the room's walls. Two straight back chairs sat in the middle of the room with a single lamp sitting on a table between them.

Carrie started acting weird again. She started feeling the seat of the chair and started to cry. I walked over to her to see what was going on.

"This is where he died. He suffered and called out for help but no one came. Someone was laughing as he sat here. I feel a pain in my chest. Like he had his heart ripped out of his body, then he just died. That was it." Carrie explained.

"His body sat here for days before anyone found him. I feel he passed but the energy is happy that he is dead. Like it had something to do with the death."

I looked at her totally confused. I trust her feelings; she has an ability that I just don't understand. But this is the most descriptive she has ever been.

"Ok, um, I guess that's all I can say."

"That picture in the other room is him," Carrie continued. "And that's his wife, he loved her very much, but he didn't trust her. And she left him; she wasn't here when he passed."

Then Carrie looked at me and fear came over her face. "Someone else is in the room. This person has pure anger. This spirit has a connection to the house but I can't figure out what."

Right then the door to the room slammed shut with a loud bang. The slam was so powerful books fell off the shelves and hit the floor. The windows rattled and dust started to be kicked up."

Carrie grabbed onto my arm and coldness fulfilled the room. The mood changed and heaviness overwhelmed us. The light that was coming in the window started to fade away. Darkness started to creep in. Then the door swung open.

"Are you two ok?" questioned Mark. "What the hell happened?"

As soon as that door opened the light came back and the heaviness went away. I looked at Carrie and the fear left her face.

"That was pretty cool wasn't it?" I said to her.

All she could do was smile at me and walk toward the door. On that note I looked at Mark, shrugged my shoulders and followed his wife to the stairs. I know he hates when she doesn't share everything with him right away. That is just how she is, mysterious.

When Carrie got to the stairs she stopped suddenly, and looked around as if others were following us. She turned and looked up the stairs and proceeded to climb them. I was right behind her pulling my flashlight out of my back pocket.

At one time I wore cargo pants on every investigation, but it seemed like I would just try to fill them all up and my legs got heavy. Now just a comfortable pair of jeans and a t-shirt is normal for me. Most of the team is the same way, but with Carrie she also wears her cross and has rosary beads in her pocket.

As we came to the top of the stairs we saw what looked like a full black mass at the end of the hallway. Chills ran down my spine and goose bumps filled my arms. It wasn't moving so I shined me light on it. A dress mannequin stood there doing nothing. What a letdown.

We started to check out the bedrooms. The first looked like the master bedroom and it was huge. It was bigger than my living room at home. A layer of dust covered the dresser and the bed. I found the light switch and turned on the lights. Two lamps on either side of the bed lit up and brightened up the room.

We looked around but nothing seemed to be touched since the invention of the vacuum. Although the bed was dusty and covered in grime you could tell that at one time this was a beautiful four poster. The only thing odd about it is that the top of the post looked like spears.

We turned the lights off and exited the room. Now down the long dark hall. We went to open the next door but it was locked so we continued down, and passed the bathroom.

We passed the bathroom with a little chuckle, because once we were called to a house to investigate a phantom smell coming from the washroom. Yeah, that was one for the books, investigating a smelly turd. But that's just some of the calls we got in the past years.

We came upon another bedroom at the end of the hall. As Carrie went into the room I looked over the banister into the open foyer. The floor which we just walked over showed a totally different look from above. Some strange symbol looking markings were on the floor.

I stared at it but dismissed it to the age of the floor. I turned and walked into the room that Carrie was in. This bedroom was just as big as the first one but you could tell that it belonged to a child at one time. I was only in there for seconds before Carrie started to head out.

Back in the hall way we saw a painting of a lady with a little girl on her lap. The girl's eyes were a bright blue and you could just see love in them. The lady on the other hand looked hard. Her eyes looked like they could melt lead, and her face was stern. It just gave you an eerie feeling, beauty and innocence being held by a hard and cold person.

Carrie stared at the picture and blurted out, "That's the girl's mother. Look there's something on the frame. Elizabeth and Tabitha Chatterley. That's strange, that's not the same woman in the picture downstairs."

"Yeah the woman down stairs is actually pretty." I said jokingly. "This woman could scare the pope."

Carrie gave me a stern look and walked away.

"What? I'm joking, Carrie come on!"

4

I caught up to Carrie half way down the stairs, and met up with the rest of the team. They were setting up command in the parlor and unpacking all the equipment.

"Ok guys we need cameras in the library, dining room, the first bedroom upstairs and the hallway upstairs. Those areas Carrie had feelings of some sort, so let's get them going."

"Yo dude, do we need drop cords up there or is there power?" Kevin asked. "Because if we need to, we've got to get them run up there without us tripping on them all night"

"Yeah there's power up there. At least in the master bedroom there is. And maybe we could just drop the camera cords off the balcony straight down to here instead of going up the stairs."

"Cool, let's go Mark. Grab the cords I have the cams and tripods." said Kevin.

They left the room and Samantha started to set up the two laptops. One laptop was to run the wireless microphone and the other is so we could download our data quickly. This way the people that are at command can start reviewing while the others are investigating.

I started to set up the digital video recorder so when the wires came down we could get them plugged in right away. The dvr is hooked up to a 32 inch flat screen monitor so we can watch that while we are at command too.

When I am stuck monitoring I try to listen to audio at the same time as I watch the monitor. Otherwise I will fall asleep or I would be on a laptop looking to tap into someone else's dsl to surf the net.

The sound of a cord hit the floor and Carrie dragged it in. And at that time I started to think we were missing someone. Where was Tammy, I haven't seen here for about an hour now.

"Has anyone seen Tammy lately?" I asked.

Both Samantha and Carrie looked up from what they were doing and I could tell that they started to think the same thing as I did.

"Ok I am going to find her. Be right back"

The girls kept setting up command and I went in search of Tammy. First place I looked was outside, but she wasn't around the cars or on the porch. This wasn't like Tammy to just wander off like this.

As I walked back into the house I checked into the library and yelled up the stairs to see if she was helping to set up the camera. Kevin said he hasn't seen her either. So I took the hallway down to the kitchen and started to walk through. There was a door open; it wasn't open during the walk through so I checked it out.

I reached for my flashlight but it wasn't in my pocket. I wish I had my cargo pants! So I did what I shouldn't do and went through the door and discovered stairs. I called Tammy's name and got no answer. So I started down the stairs.

It took a while to get down the stairs in the dark, but every couple stairs I called out Tammy's name hoping she would call back. As I got to the bottom of the stairs I felt something hit my head. It was a pull cord for a light, and I pulled it.

The bulb flickered a little then lit up all the way. I gave a quick look around and called her name again. A mouse ran across the floor but there were no other movements. So I ventured through the basement further. Mostly it was empty except for the boiler and electrical boxes.

There was a room to the right which I thought was the old coal room since it was the only room that matched the rest of the foundation walls. I stuck my head in as I walked passed.

With my shock I saw what looked like a person sitting in the corner of the room. So I walked in. It was Tammy and she was in a fetal position in the corner. I knelt down and put my had on her arm.

She turned her head and screamed so loud I thought my fillings were going to fall out. My head moved back from the scream as her hand came into contact with my cheek and scratched me.

I could not really see her in the dark so I tried to comfort her explaining it was me. To no avail she continued slapping and clawing at me. Screaming as she did this, I pushed back from her and she just kept screaming.

Through the doorway bouncing lights came rolling in, it was Mark and Kevin.

"What the hell!" Kevin said as they entered the room. His flashlight beamed solely on Tammy. As I looked at her, I saw her clothes were torn and she was dirty. She was as dirty as a mineworker. Her eyes were distant and look like she was crying.

"Tammy its Kevin, are you ok?" he said in a way you would try to talk to someone that doesn't speak English. "What happened to you?"

She glared at him, like she could see right through him. And she didn't speak a word. At least she didn't scream at him like she did me.

Mark came over to me and helped me off the floor. As I brushed myself off he told me I was bleeding. I reached up and felt my cheek. I could feel the wetness and when I pulled my hand away there was a little blood on my hand. But my concern at that time was Tammy.

Kevin continued to console Tammy but as he stood up she bit him on his leg. He jumped back and she stood up and stared at all of us.

"Son of a....she bit me!" said a shocked Kevin.

My attention was brought back to Tammy and she started to run out the door, but she tripped and hit her head on the door frame, she was out cold.

Mark walked over to her, and picked her up. We all left the room a little bothered with what happened. Kevin complained that he got bit all the way to the stairs. When we reached the base of the stairs I looked up and Samantha and Carrie were at the top waiting for word.

"Grab the first aid kit, she's hurt." I called up.

We climbed the stairs, Tammy still not moving in Marks arms. We headed right for the parlor. Mark laid Tammy on the couch and Carrie sat next to her.

I told everyone what happened and all of us were taken aback about the whole situation. For the most part this was uncharacteristic of Tammy and we couldn't understand why she was acting like this.

Sam walked back into the room and had the first aid kit already open. As she put it down Carrie grabbed the ice pack and activated it. She put it on Tammy's head.

"I am calling for an ambulance." proclaimed Kevin. "She needs help."

Ok, Kevin taking charge is like a dog trying to pee on a cactus. It may work but it's going to hurt.

He pulled the phone away from his ear and said, "My battery died. Dude can I use your phone?"

I rolled my eyes back and reached in my pocket for my phone. He probably thought they would charge him for his minutes.

"No don't." a tired voice interrupted. It was Tammy, "I am ok."

Kevin pocketed his phone and walked over to the couch and sat down on the arm. He strokes her hair caringly and looked down at her.

"Why in the hell did you bite me?"

Yeah Kevin is one of those people that don't think before they speak. There is no filter between his brain and mouth. This woman has knocked herself out and all he thinks of is why she bit him. Of course, I would like to know too.

"What do you mean? I found the door in the kitchen so I decided to go check out the basement. When I got to the bottom of the stairs I saw the light. I pulled the cord but nothing. So I went to check out down there with just my flashlight. Then I heard a voice calling my name. I thought it was you Mike. So I walked towards it."

"As I passed the room on the right I got pushed into the wall. Whatever it was, I never heard footsteps or anything. I tried to push off the wall and lost my balance. Then I was pulled into that room. After that I don't know what happened. I woke up here."

Well now isn't this a fine sack of potatoes. We have a team member that was just attacked and still the owner wasn't here. What did I get us into?

5

After fifteen minutes of arguing on whether we pack up or continue Tammy was the deciding vote on staying. She was banged up and confused but willing to go on. I care about my team, and my friends, but I was still thinking of the five grand.

We split into two teams and got the cameras up and recording. Kevin had to be the one to do a test check on the walkie talkies, one in each and against his face, so the feedback was loud and annoying.

My team was Samantha, Carrie and myself as usual. And of course Mark had to tell me the rules of investigating with his wife. This of course happened every time we did this. He gave her a kiss and we were on our way

Carrie brought out her dowsing rods as we headed upstairs. Dowsing rods are not scientific but strangely enough they work just like a normal emf meter. The copper rods must become magnified from the energy around it. But I had our meter just to make sure.

Samantha carried the non-contact thermometer and voice recorder. I had a high def camcorder and the emf meter. I started recording and asked where we should go. Carrie insisted to go upstairs and check out the master bedroom first.

"Now, remember to be respectful and none provoking, we don't need another attack tonight." Carrie continued to lecture me on this and I agreed.

See spirits were at one time human and just like everyone else. Now that they are on the other side, the only difference is that they don't have a body. So when I start taunting they react just like anyone else.

We followed Carrie up the stairs, and I could tell that Sam was really freaked out. I never saw her like this and I started to get concerned. I know that this is the first time that someone on our team got attacked this bad, but we had a job to do.

I moved a little faster so I could grab her hand and she gave my hand a real hard squeeze. The tension was just starting to ease as we got up stairs. We made the turn into the bedroom.

"I feel that he is in here with us, and he is scared." Carrie said.

"Ok Sam start recording and I will take some temperature readings."

Carrie sat on the bed and put one rod in each hand and started to ask questions. The theory is a spirit can move the rods to communicate with the person holding them. Usually they just cross but sometimes she asks them to move them one way or the other to answer yes or no questions.

I walked around checking if there are any drafts or temperature differences so we have a definite base line. Then I sat down on the floor next to a chair in the corner, yes I know I am difficult to understand. I got Carrie into focus with the camcorder and opened up my senses.

"Is there anyone here with us tonight? If so please come near me." said Carrie. "I feel you here so please come close, we won't hurt you."

Nothing happened, so she tried again. Within seconds of her asking the temperature dropped and the rods crossed. I picked up the emf meter and slid it towards her and instantly it went off.

"Are you a man or a woman?" she asked. "Move the rods to the right for man, left for woman."

They moved to the right, and I caught the moving on cam as well as the security cams set up in the room. With the light going off on the meter it just was backing up the experience.

"Thank you. Now to answer yes move the rods to the left and for no move them to the right. If you understand move them to the left."

They moved to the left. If it was me I would be confused. Did she mean her left or mine. It's just one of those questions that could go either way. I made sure that I kept

Carrie in frame as I set the camcorder down on the chair.

"Thank you. Did you use to live here?"

Once again they moved to the left. And at the same time the meter lit up. This is great evidence we are collecting. If only we could get this every time we go out.

"Thank you. Did you attack Tammy down in the basement?"

They moved to the right, and the meter went off. Ok it's the first time that it moved that way. Then I thought again what if the other questions were no and the last one was yes. Well anyways...

"Is there more than one spirit in this house?" Carrie asked. They moved left. "Are they near us?"

They moved to the right so at least we knew that there was only one spirit in the room at that time.

"Are they in the basement?"

Nothing happened on either the emf meter or the rods. The feeling in the room began to change. A depressing feeling started to come over me. It also looked like the room got darker. The temperature dropped, it felt like 10 degrees.

At the same time the rods crossed and the meter started going off. Then the rods just started to spin in circles never in my life have I ever seen that!

"Hello?" Carrie said in a nervous tone. "Can you stop touching my rods please?"

The rods stopped, and they flew out of Carries hands and hit the wall across the room. Drawers of the dresser started to rattle then open.

"Holy crap!" yelled Sam

"Ok we got to get out of here!" I said grabbing Sam's hand pulling her off the floor. "Carrie lets go. Come on!"

She just sat there. The meter was still going off. I reached out to her and pulled her off the bed. As I did that it felt like I stuck my arm in a freezer. I lead the girls out the door and the drawers in the dresser started to come all the way out and hit the floor.

The cams set in there are recording all of this. So I didn't care much if we didn't capture it on the hand held. We made our way to the stairs.

"Did you all see that? It was freaking incredible!" I told the rest of the group.

"What are you talking about?" Mark said. "The rods moving or the meter going off?"

"The drawers, the rods flying, all the crap that just happened. Move over bro!"

Mark moved and I sat down in front of the monitor. I stopped recording and started rewinding. When I got to the point where we walked in I hit play. What makes this boring is we couldn't afford the dvr system with sound so all we could do is just watch.

"Ok there's where the rods started crossing and me sliding the meter over and it started flashing. Left, left, right, and left. Ok now it's coming up."

I motioned to the group to come closer. I could see Sam and Carrie sat down on the couch not wanting to see. Then the meter went off and nothing. The rods just fell out of Carrie's hands and dropped to the floor. Then you just see us there looking around, then getting up and running out.

What the hell! What about the drawers. All that crap flying around, and hitting the floor, but nothing, not even a dust orb appeared.

"Swear to god man, the dressers opened and flew just as far as Carries rods."

"Dude we were wondering why you guys were freaking out. I thought it was a spider!" Kevin chimed in.

See Kevin is scared the death of spiders. He had a tarantula put on him and that was it. He started screaming like a little girl and ran away. Found out later that he wet himself in the process. Yes, tales of the pet store.

"Kevin, Mark come with me and let's check it out." I said.

They grabbed flashlights and we headed upstairs. I slowed down and let them pass me as we got to the room. As they went in I took a deep breath and followed. I looked around, and nothing was out of place except for the meter with the rods lying next to it.

Did we all imagine what happen? A group hallucination. I just don't understand. Everything that happened to us, no proof at all, how can that be?

We walked back downstairs and back to the women. Very unsure of ourselves, we started to ask Carrie and Sam what they experienced. To Kevin and Mark's surprise they stories were the same as mine. Right down to the drawers flying out of the dresser.

"If all that happened, why didn't the cameras pick it up? They we recording and we saw everything that happened. It was nothing. You guy just imagined everything." The sarcasm in Kevin's voice was truly annoying.

So I went back and started to rewind the video and check again. I stopped and started playing it at the point when we walked in. It was on full screen and I watched attentively. I didn't even blink for a few minutes in fear I would miss something.

Mark and Kevin started to pick up equipment to start their investigations. Tammy still was shaken up and elected to stay at command with us. The guys on the other hand were going back to the bedroom. I myself had to watch the video, for anything out of the ordinary, just something.

6

Samantha sat down in the chair beside me and wrapped her arms around me. I was so involved in watching the video I didn't even notice how concerned she was. She had the same experience as I did, so she was probably as freaked as I was.

"Babe, I know what I saw, I know what you saw. But we just didn't catch it." she said to me. "Did you check your camcorder?"

Crap! I forgot the camcorder upstairs. We left in such a hurry I just left it on the chair. And the good thing is that it was recording; now I just got to pull myself together and go get it.

"What's that?" I asked while pointing to the monitor. "Look right there, behind Carrie. See that shadow?"

There was a shadow form behind Carrie, and at that moment the rods crossed. Then the screen went fuzzy and we weren't in the room. I backed the video up a bit and watched again. This time I noticed the time stamp. Ten minutes were missing from the recording.

"Hey Mark, did you guys pause the video?" I called over the walkie talkie. "Mark come in. Mark?" No answer.

"Ok they aren't answering. I am going to go up there and grab the camcorder and ask them."

"You want me to go with you?" said Sam.

"No I'll be fine. It will only take a couple minutes. Can you start recording on the dvr again? I'll be right back."

I grabbed my flashlight and gave Sam a kiss on the forehead. I looked over at Tammy and gave her a little wink and smile. I started towards the door and Carrie stood by the door.

"Let's go." she said to me. "I am going with and don't try to stop me."

Well I guess I got company going up there. I think she wanted some questions answered too. So why not? It would be safer and although I wouldn't say it out loud, but I was still a little freaked.

"HEY!"

We all jumped as Kevin opened the door. Sometimes he could be a complete tool; he always tried to scare us. This time I about messed myself.

"Kevin! What in the hell is your problem?" Samantha said.

"What I just came back to get batteries. Our voice recorder died on us so I ran down to grab some."

"Well you scared the hell out of us you fuck!" commented Tammy.

"Some ghost hunters you all are. Scared by an opening door!" said Kevin trying to hold in his laughter.

"Kev, did you or Mark pause or stop the dvr while we were upstairs?" I asked and by the look on his face I already knew his answer.

"No man, we sat here talking, didn't touch the dvr at all. Why?"

"We lost ten minutes of video. The time jumped and there is no explanation."

Kevin then walked over to the monitor and started flipping through its menu. He probably was seeing if the time lapse was on or not. Or maybe to just check the system to make sure that it was running correctly.

"All this looks good, I don't know bro maybe there was a glitch. I will check it out when I get home." Kevin muttered.

He got out of the menu and looked at the monitor. It was on the four screens; this way when someone is sitting there they can see all the cameras at once. But in one of the cameras, there was something out of place. In the bedroom, where is Mark?

"I left Mark in the bedroom. He was sitting on the bed when I came down to get the batteries." said Kevin. "Maybe he is on his way down."

At that point a few things all happened at once. First a loud bang came from the other side of the door, loud enough to rattle the hinges. Second the girls all screamed at the same time. That surprised me more than the bang.

And the big one, the camera that was in the bedroom went completely black. There was still a video feed but there was no picture. Then the video was back on like nothing was wrong.

"Something must have fallen and hit the cables. We better check them and make sure the cams are not going to lose feed." I commented. "Kevin, I will go back up with you and we can check it all out. Carrie you stay here with Sam and Tammy."

We all agreed and Kevin and I headed out the door. As we walked to the stairs we were shining our flashlight on the cables making sure they were clear.

As we came to the stairs we looked up and saw a quick moving black mass. A black mass is a figure with no features and totally dark. It's like light is absorbed through this thing and no light would pass. The mass moved so fast down the stairs we couldn't follow it with our eyes.

Kevin sighed as I did because this is another experience not captured on tape. This is our luck and hopefully we will capture something today. But right now we have to make sure the cables are all good.

As we got to the top of the stairs and Kevin called out to Mark. Still no answer, what the hell! Mark never plays tricks on anyone. In fact it's hard to realize that he had a sense of humor. Kevin called out to him again and silence echoed through the house.

As we approached the bedroom I swear I heard laughing coming from down stairs. The bad thing is it didn't sound like any of the girls. Although it was a woman's laugh, it sounded odd in some way.

We went into the bedroom and it was empty. Mark was nowhere in sight. The equipment was there but he wasn't. So I grabbed my camcorder and started to look around the room.

Kevin headed to the hall and started to check out the other rooms on that floor. He discovered that all the rooms where empty. Now that we are both scratching our heads wondering where this guy was, we headed back to the main floor to check around there.

As we got off the stairs Carrie came out and asked where Mark was. We answered her honestly and she went to the front door to check if we went outside. As she opened the door a cold breeze passed us. The weird thing is it went to the door, not come from the door.

Carrie jumped back as the wind blew to her and the door slammed. The sound of the lock echoed through the hall. Kevin ran to the door and tried to open it but it wouldn't open.

"Dude this is bullshit. How are we going to get out?" Kevin said in a panic.

"Come on if the lock is stuck we will just go out the back door. Don't fucking go nuts. All you're going to do is scare the girls."

"Bro, you saw shit and Tammy did too. Mark is missing, and we need to get out of here."

"Mike, I have to agree. Let's find Mark and leave." said Carrie.

"As soon as Mrs. Chatterley gets here we will leave, but I gave my word. We can't go until she gets here and we tell her what happened and get our money."

"Screw the money!" said Kevin. "We need to get out of here. I don't like this crap and we need an exorcist or something!"

Carrie came closer to me and looked in my eyes and just said a few words that made me really think. "One down."

7

We all looked at Carrie in shock, not for what she said but for the way she looked. She had a glazed look on her face and she was pale. Her voice was raspy and she sounded like she has the flu.

"What do you mean one down? Dude what the hell is she talking about, one down!"

"Kev chill. Carrie are you ok? Do you know where you are?" I tried to make sense of the situation. I kept asking Carrie what's going on but she just stood there.

"Carrie, where is your cross?"

Finally her head moved down and she looked at her cross, and then looked back up with an evil smile on her face. Then she collapse and she fell to the floor. Sam and Kevin helped her up to her feet.

"Oh my god! I know. We need to go upstairs." Carrie said softly. "We need to get in the room that's locked. We need to get in there now!"

"Why Carrie? What's going on? You got to tell us what the hell happened to you!" I said. "We are not going to do anything until you tell us."

"Mike you need to trust me. First you and Kevin need to go downstairs and get Mark. He is in the coal room where you found Tammy. Then we all will go upstairs together." Carrie continued. "The clues are in that bedroom and I think that's where we will figure this all out."

"Fine, Kev let's go."

"Fuck that, I am getting my ass out of here! This is all freaking me out! Mark disappears and Tammy is attacked. And

Carrie looks like she was possessed by Betty White with a head cold!" Kevin was freaking out, and this was the first time any of us witnessed his panic. It's like a spider crawled up his face and fell asleep on his nose. "And you know what, fuck this ghost hunting shit! All fun and games till someone gets hurt."

"Kevin stay here." interrupted Samantha. "I will go with Mike and get Mark. Then we will talk about getting out of here. But you need to stay with Tammy and Carrie. You need to protect them. Ok?"

"Yeah but I am out of here no matter what!"

Sam and I grabbed a couple of flashlights and headed out of the room. We have been a group for years and never have my team been scared. Also this is the first time Sam took charge. She usually stood back and took everything in, just following directions.

Sam took lead through the kitchen to the stairway.

"Ok the door is still open," she commented. "So let's head down."

"Are you ok?" I asked, worried about her mindset.

"Yeah let's just get down there and find Mark and get out of here."

We headed down the stairs and called out Marks name. The silence was so loud it was deafening. About half way down we heard a voice, a man's voice. It was Marks voice and he was calling for us.

We hurried to find him. We got to the coal room and in the same corner that Tammy was in there sat Mark. Dirty and looking confused Mark stood up and slowly walked towards us.

"I don't know what happened or how I got here. All I know is Kevin said he was going down to get batteries and the room got cold. So I started to ask questions. Next thing I know I saw a shadow come in the room. It walked up to me and touched my leg." Mark continued. "At first I thought it was cool, but then whatever it was grabbed my leg and pulled me. Then it was like all the air was knocked out of me and my chest hurt."

Ok this is a pretty good story. But how did he get down stairs and why didn't he let us know. Of all the years Mark and I have known each other; he never has lied to me, so why would he start now?

"I tried to grab on to something and I couldn't get a grip on anything. The pain in my chest started getting stronger, and I blacked out." Mark wiped some dirt off his face. "I woke up when I heard your voice."

"You scared the crap out of us bro! Kevin is crapping his pants over all of this."

"Yeah now let's get out of here." voiced Sam. "We are leaving."

"How did you find me?" asked Mark.

"Your wife went into some kind of trance and said you were down here. Kevin didn't want to come down with me so Sam volunteered."

"This is the reason I can't do anything without her knowing. She sees everything." Said Mark.

We turned and headed for the door. I started to think about what he just said and now I really wonder about Carrie's abilities. What are they and how do they work. Does she know everything that is happening around us? How did she know exactly where Mark was at?

I led us to the stairs and we started up. Sam started up first and I followed Mark in case he blacked out again.

As we exited the stairwell, I noticed that there were blood stains on Mark's shirt. I stopped him and turned him around to see a huge rip in the chest of his shirt. I pulled up his shirt and huge scratches encircled the area where his heart was.

"Mark do you remember this happening?" I asked.

His response was a simple no as he looked at his chest. Unshaken he pulled his shirt down and continued on to command. Sam gave me a worried look and followed him. I stood there trying to comprehend everything that has happened so far. Now I am more confused then when we got here.

8

When I got back to command I saw Carrie holding Mark as if he returned from war. A small tear trickled down her face and although I couldn't hear what she was saying, I knew.

Now that the whole team was together we needed to decide whether to stay, leave, or wait outside for the old lady to get here. I couldn't just pack up and leave but I was not sure what everyone else was feeling.

"Ok everyone I know that some of you want to go," Carrie said, "but I think I know where we can find all the answers to what's going on."

She started to tell us why and I looked around to see how everyone was taking in this news. Most had a look like they were going to kill her.

"I heard the voice of a man. He said that all the answers to the house are in the locked bedroom. We wouldn't be able to leave until we know the source and beat it."

I had to speak up. "I know we are going through hell with this, but I put my trust in Carrie. I think we need to go up there and see what's going on"

"Screw that!" said Kevin. "I vote that we pack our shit up and get out of here!"

"I think we should stay." commented Tammy. "I am scared but I need to know what happened to me. I would be questioning everything in life until I know. Kevin please, I need to know!"

"Dude you were attacked and dragged into a coal room. Look at Mark, he was attacked too and neither of you know what happened. Mark doesn't wanna stay, why would you?"

"I want to know too." said Mark. He spoke more in a calm mono tone voice. I guess because he was still trying to make sense of the events so far.

"Come on your all fucking nuts! Can't you see that whatever is here doesn't want us here? The old lady set us up!"

"Kevin," I interrupted, "calm down. Listen we all will be together, both attacks happened when someone was alone. Nothing will happen to us. I promise."

Kevin gave me a look that would melt steel. He then walked towards the couch and sat down. He rested his head in his hands and elbows on his knees. I could tell he was going to stay. He shook his head and looked up.

"Ok man, but we leave after checking out that room."

We all agreed, well I thought so. Sam looked scared and didn't want to go. I pulled her into my arms and held her tight. Whispering into her ear words of encouragement she whispered something back. She was pregnant.

Now for the first time I was scared too. Not only am I putting the woman I love on the line but my unborn…..baby. Wait didn't she tell me she had her period earlier?

"What do you mean?"

Sam looked up at me and said, "Charles I am pregnant."

Who is Charles?

I took a deep look at Sam; she had a glow to her that I never saw before. She looked absolutely beautiful. She was always beautiful but never like this. Maybe I am going to be a dad.

As Sam and I talked the rest of the team grabbed equipment and started to head for the door. I had a very hard time taking my eyes off of Samantha, but I had to. I reached out for her hand and led her to the door.

I had so many mixed feelings going through my head. Now I am doubting our decision. Although that five grand would help, tomorrow I really need to find a job, now more than ever.

As we got to the stairs I looked at Sam and she didn't look the same. Very strange, the glow disappeared. Now she looks tired and scared.

"Are you ok?"

"Yeah fine."

"When did you find out that you were pregnant?"

"I am not pregnant. Where did you come up with that?"

Ok now I really needed to stop and get Carrie over here. Not even five minutes ago this woman told me that she was going to have a baby and now she's not.

I asked Carrie to walk with us and explained what just happened and she said "I know." She then went on to tell us for a brief moment that a spirit entered Sam and used her as a way to talk to us. Sam immediately went white, now this is the Sam I know.

9

The group headed up the stairs towards the locked room. As we got to the door Mark reached out and tried again to open the door, still locked.

Then Kevin summoned the spirit of Bruce Lee and started some weird karate warm up. Then he planted his feet, and with a solid kick, fell on his ass. With a sigh I looked at him as everyone started to laugh. Finally a moment tonight that lightened the mood.

Tammy grabbed the doorknob and turned it and the door opened. She pushed it open and we all looked in. unbelievably this is the only room that was clean and neat.

With pride Kevin got up smiling thinking he kicked the door in. He pulled up his pants and walked in. The rest of us followed him in shaking our heads.

Samantha found a light switch and turned on the lights. This room was magnificent. A large canopy bed with lace draped around it, the bedding was tight and not one wrinkle in it. Queen Anne type furniture accompanied the bed. Two bedside tables flanked the bed, and a large dresser sat at the wall in front of the bed.

We walked around checking everything out and Samantha saw a book on one of the tables. She sat down on the bed and opened it. It was a diary. It was Mrs. Chatterley's diary. One by one we gathered around Sam as she started to read.

She began with the date, March twenty sixth eighteen sixty four. Oddly this must be the great grandmother of the old lady that hired us. But the book didn't look a hundred and fifty years old.

In the book she talked about her wedding day, and how deeply in love she was with her husband Charles. We found out it was an arranged marriage, one that was made by their parents a decade earlier. The Chatterley's were wealthy and her parents came to the country poor and worked hard to make ends meet. Her father needed money to start a small business, and went to the Chatterley's for a loan. The Chatterley's owned a textile business and were the wealthiest people in the area. In exchange for the loan they agreed that their oldest daughter would marry the Chatterley's eldest son.

This secured their families future, marrying into the towns richest family. This dream wouldn't last long. When Elizabeth was fourteen, her family's house burnt down, killing her parents and older sister. With the agreement of the marriage the Chatterley's brought her into the house and raised her to the age of eighteen. At that point she married their son Charles.

Although she was deeply in love with Charles he did not feel the same way. He despised his parents for arranging the marriage and did not treat her with much respect. They were married but didn't show it. But when it was time to do her wifely duties she felt the most love, but when it was over he left her alone.

Years went by and she became pregnant. She told the news to Charles hoping he would be happy. He sighed and slapped her. This destroyed her, she ran upstairs crying. Days later he came to her apologizing for his actions.

It seemed her pregnancy brought them closer together; they started attending events together where he went alone before. They smiled and laughed, all seemed great.

Nine months passed and they welcomed in a girl to their family. They named her Tabitha. They had a happy little family, until five years later.

At the age of five young Tabitha contracted small pox. The house was quarantined and their baby died a month later. After her daughter's death Elizabeth went into a deep depression. She locked herself in her room and would cry for hours.

Another blow to them happened a year later with the deaths of Charles parents a month apart. Elizabeth did not attend the funerals. Charles inherited the family business and was set for life.

For years Elizabeth blamed herself for her daughter's death, and became secluded within the walls of her room. Two years after the death of Tabitha, Charles entered her room and told her that he met a woman and was going to marry her. But first she had to go.

This was the final blow to Elizabeth, already in a state of depression, she could not handle this news and screamed and cried openly. Begging Charles to reconsider they were unheard. Charles packed her clothing and was ready to throw her out.

At this point the writing in the book changed. It wasn't Elizabeth hand writing anymore. In the second paragraph of the new person's writings we found out that Sarah was the new wife of Charles.

After packing all of Elizabeth's clothes, Charles grabbed her arm to throw her out. But she broke free and ran out of the room and threw herself over the banister, landing in the foyer below.

Two months after the funeral Charles married Sarah and she moved into the house. They kept Elizabeth's room locked and the way it was at the time of her death.

Years went by and Sarah never felt at home. She begged Charles to move and he always said no. It was his family's house and he wasn't going to move. Sarah began to see and hear things, all unexplained.

Just after their fifth anniversary she couldn't take it anymore and left Charles and the house.

10

"That's where it ends," Sam said.

"Well it explains what happened here but how is this clues to our case?" I asked. "This explains a few things but what about the ghost that killed her husband?"

"Well hold on let's get back to command and let me run a check on Charles," said Tammy

We all went down stairs and Tammy sat in front of a laptop, tapped into someone's dsl and did a search on these people. Within a few minutes she found something.

"Here we go, Charles Chatterley heir to Chatterley Textiles died October seventh eighteen ninety nine. He was alone and broke, the business closed two years earlier. They say he was murdered and his heart was cut out while he was in the library."

Ok this coincides with what Carrie said when we first went into the library. So once again we have proof to back up Carrie.

"He was found in the chair but his heart was found in the coal room downstairs. With the thick dust in the basement no footprints were found. Though Sarah was never found, she wasn't a suspect, and the case was never solved."

We all took all this in and wondered. I could tell most of us were in awe over all of this, but Kevin was showing he wanted to go.

"Well we still haven't solved anything." said Mark. "But with that said what are we going to do?"

"I know what I am going to do, leave." exclaimed Kevin. "We know that the Sarah chick killed the old man and took off. Now let's get out of here!"

"But how do we know Kev? There is no proof. We need…."

"No Tammy we *need* to get the hell out of here! I am leaving here with or without you!"

He started to gather his things as we all tried to talk him into staying. To no avail he opted to leave, and walked out of the parlor.

I went after him to talk to him in private, but as he reached the door and tried to open it, it wouldn't open. He pulled and pulled and nothing. I even tried to help him and it wouldn't budge.

"That's it!" He yelled and he dropped his bag. As he turned around I had a bad feeling. Kevin ran up the stairs yelling.

Everyone came out of the parlor to see what was happening. Mark looked at me and we both ran up the stairs after him. As we got to the top of the stairs we couldn't believe what we saw. Kevin was in the hall in front of the first bedroom yelling at the spirit to let him out.

Everything happened so fast. Kevin was screaming, "Let me out you fucking psycho ghost bitch…..I want out!" Then it happened, a shadow appeared at the banister and with speed I couldn't describe it hit Kevin and pushed him into the room. We ran over to the doorway and as we got there we watched Kevin get pushed through the second story window. As he fell the broken shards of glass then came flying back into the room.

We ducked and covered our heads to avoid getting cut. Seconds later we stood up and looked in the room. Kevin was gone and the window……..was intact. Not even a scratch or crack.

Mark and I looked at each other and at the same time said, "The basement!"

We turned around and raced down the stairs. Taking the stairs two at a time we got to the bottom and made the left turn towards the kitchen. We passed the women without saying a word but they knew and followed. We got to the stairs leading to the basement and turned on our flashlights.

We flew down the stairs and made our way to the coal room. When we got there and looked in we saw….nothing. Kevin wasn't there, we looked through the room and he wasn't there.

Mark and I turned and exited out of the room. The walk back took what seemed like forever. Although Kevin had a few faults, he was a close friend and now he is gone. The bad thing is we did not know where.

As we went up the stairs we did not speak. We didn't know what to say, and we didn't know what to tell the women. How can you tell someone you watched your friend fly out a window and the window fixed itself?

At the top of the stairs we joined the women and I put my arm around Sam and walked back to command. When we all got back into the room Mark and I sat down and told what happened.

Carrie and Sam both started to cry as Mark and I comforted them. It really hit them, and then I realized Tammy wasn't with us. Now where the hell did she go?

"Where the hell is Tammy?" I questioned.

Not one of us knew where she was or when she disappeared. We have to find her and quick. But we have to stay together; it's not safe being alone.

11

Now with Tammy missing and Kevin gone we are all on edge. But we have to be strong and find Tammy. We picked up our flashlights and emf meter and headed out of the parlor. We entered the foyer in a pack.

We walked through the dining room and kitchen and no sign of her. Also no one in the basement, these are all the places that we found to be the most odd.

We went back into the foyer and feared the idea of going upstairs. So I led us into the library and there was Tammy.

Her shirt was ripped open and her hands were bound to the chair. Blood covered her torn bra and a gaping hole was in her chest where her heart would be. She is dead.

Sam screamed and Carrie buried her head into Marks chest. I walked over to Tammy's body and closed her eyes. Mark let go of Carrie and helped me free her hands. We picked her up off the chair and laid her out on the floor. Tammy was such a warm and caring person that will be missed greatly. Especially by me.

Mark walked out of the room and took a sheet off some furniture and brought it back in to the room. We all said a silent prayer and covered our fallen friend. I could barely see with the tears in my eyes and I could see Marks eye welling up as well.

We slowly walked out of the library, turning the light off as we left. Slowly we walked back into the parlor and sat down. No one spoke for what seemed like an hour.

Then I noticed something on the monitor. Upstairs it looked like a woman walking out of the bedroom that was locked. I watched the figure move down the hall and the figure went out of frame.

I picked the figure up again as it went through the dining room. And again out of picture. I mentioned it to Mark and he said we should check it out. Then we calmly convinced the women to go with us.

When we got into the kitchen we noticed the door going downstairs was closed. We kept that door open all night and this is the first time that we saw it closed.

Mark opened it and we turned our flashlights on and started downstairs. Cautiously we made it to the coal room, and shined our lights in there. Then a blood curdling scream that came from Sam's mouth. The reason is because we found Tammy's heart.

This was all that we could all stand; the pain involved in this was too strong to bear. We had to solve this so we could get our asses out of here and call the police in. We needed to get Tammy's body to her family and we still needed to fine Kevin.

Mark pulled Carrie and Samantha out of the room as I thought about picking up the heart. I couldn't pull enough strength together to do it and I felt like a piece of shit because I couldn't, so I turned to exit the room.

When we got back into the parlor Sam walked up to me and slapped me hard in the face.

"You always got to take the easy way out. Never thinking about others. Because of you wanting fame and fortune in the paranormal business we lost two friends tonight. Why won't you ever grow the fuck up?"

Deep down I knew she was right. After seeing all those shows on TV I thought why couldn't we do that? I guess I lived in a fantasy world, and didn't want to leave it.

Ghost Hunted

All I could say was sorry and I knew that wasn't good enough. Now I really needed to think of a way to get us out of this house. Then I thought about breaking a window. There were large windows in the parlor and library, if we broke them we could climb out.

I told the idea to Mark and he agreed. So I picked up a chair and threw it through a window. It shattered and glass littered the floor. With a halfhearted smile I walked to it and as I got a few feet away the shutters closed shutting us back in.

With this Mark ran to the library and the shutters closed there too. Once again we were stuck. It was getting old, and another idea came to me.

12

My idea is simple, use Carrie to talk to this spirit and find out what we need to do to get out of here. Her being sensitive might be our ticket out.

"Carrie this is my plan. We are going to go upstairs and I need to make contact with this thing and see why it's keeping us here." I continued. "I don't care how you do it but this might be our last hope."

"Mike, I don't know if I can. I will try but I just don't know."

We all said a prayer, and grabbed her stuff and started to go back up stairs. All of us were frightened, but we have to keep going. Step by step we get closer to getting out of here.

We decided to go in the clean room and that's where we started. Hopefully we could make contact with a friendlier spirit. The feeling in the room is probably the best of the house. A lot of the rooms just seem heavy, but here in this room it seemed better. But that was just my opinion.

After thirty minutes we got bunk, Carrie sensed nothing. It started to seem like a waste of time so Mark suggested going to another room. And again nothing, there is only one room left. And we all dreaded going in there.

We entered the room and it was cold, the air was heavy. The depressed feeling encircled all of us. Carrie had her dowsing rods out and started to ask questions and got a quick response.

"Are you a man?" she asked and the rods went to the left. "Is your name Charles?"

Again the rods went to the left. So this spirit is Mr. Chatterley. Clearly this is not the same entity that has been causing the problems we have had tonight. Carrie continued to ask questions and got responses.

The biggest question that she asked was if Sarah killed him and the answer was no.

Then the air got colder and the responses ended. Carrie tried to get them to talk some more but it was done with him. But she sensed another presence.

"What is your name?" Carrie asked. "I demand you answer me."

I never have seen Carrie get so disrespectful. But she was digging and she was working hard. She had a purpose and you could tell. Then she said something I didn't expect.

"Elizabeth, why did you kill Charles?"

Then I saw the scariest thing ever. Right behind Carrie something started to manifest. It was a female and it looked pissed.

"Answer me Elizabeth," commanded Carrie.

"For the same reason I will kill you." it said.

Carrie turned and saw the spirit and it screamed at her. It reminded me of what a banshee is supposed to sound like. Mark went to move towards Carrie but didn't get there soon enough and she was dragged out of the room. We ran after, and I watched as Carrie went flying over the rail.

Mark grabbed her hand at the last moment barely holding on to her. The strain showed across his face, and he tried to pull her back up over the rail.

He started to pull her up, but only holding her with one hand is hard even for a bodybuilder. So he let go of the rail and reached down with his other hand and started to lift her up. When her head was level with his shoulders, the rail creaked and fell.

Mark and Carrie both fell crashing to the foyer floor below. As I stepped to the edge I could see their bodies lying there, still holding hands, forever.

13

Still in shock, Sam and I made our way down the stairs. I was in total disbelief and held back tears. Samantha on the other hand was crying hysterically. Not only did we lose our best friends but our last chance of getting out. We knelt down next to our friends, and that's when I finally lost it.

After five minutes I finally wiped the tears from my face and stood up. I helped Sam off the floor and pulled her into a tight embrace. This could be our last moments together; I wasn't going to lose the chance to hold her as long as I could.

We walked through the foyer and back into the parlor. I looked around at our equipment and thought it wasn't worth it. Maybe it never was I thought we were helping people and in turn we lost friends, happiness and now I fear, our lives.

Samantha sat on a couch trying to pull herself together, but still I could feel her body shake every time she was about to stop crying. I myself felt numb, doubting everything I have done in the past five years.

I should have found a good job, married Sam and raised a family. Instead I followed a childhood dream which turned into the worse decision I have ever made.

"Mike, what are we going to do? I want to go. I don't want to die."

"I don't know babe, I really don't know."

I looked at my watch and knew the sun would be coming up soon. We have been here all night. Now I really need to figure a way out. And still I can't figure anything out. Wait, we still never tried the backdoor. We talked about it but never tried.

I stood up slowly and looked through the dvr cameras to see if I could see the back door in one. And I could barely see it behind the open door in the kitchen. Since the door to the basement was open most of the night we forgot about it.

"Sam I have an idea. We need to run to the kitchen and try the back door. I am afraid this is our last chance"

She agreed but I didn't think she was too optimistic. She has been through a lot and saw things that we never thought would happen. Her face was dirty and you can see trails where tears streamed down her cheeks.

"*Mike,*" a voice said. I knew it wasn't Sam; I was looking right at her.

"Did you hear that? Someone said my name." I said to Sam.

"No, I didn't." she replied.

Great now I am going crazy. Hearing voices, what's next? Me running through the house with a knife trying to stab a ghost. I need to pull myself together and get Sam out of here.

"*Mike trust me I will get you out.*" This voice is familiar, but it seems so far away. "*You always have trusted me; though my body is gone I am still with you. You need to trust me and do what I say. Please for Samantha.*"

Holy crap its Carrie, how is this possible? I walked to the door leading to the foyer and looked out and their bodies were still there. I turned quickly and looked at Sam.

"The voice is Carrie's, she is here."

Sam started to walk towards me and said, "Mike, Carrie is gone."

She reached out to me and grabbed my hand. Maybe she's right and finally I snapped. But maybe if I ask the voice to do something it would be proof.

"Carrie…..if that is you please do something to prove it is you."

A few seconds past and I asked again. "Carrie please…..show yourself."

Samantha again had a tear in her eye just forming. She thinks I'm gone and I believe I am with her on that one. Then over Sam's shoulder I see something on the monitor. It's Carrie on the second floor.

"Sam, look…..camera two."

Sam turned around and saw the same figure on the screen. I enlarged the cameras view so it filled the screen. And with a sigh Sam saw Carrie's face on top of the figure.

14

"I don't believe it. Carrie is up stairs!" screamed Sam as she turned and ran to the door. Then screamed again as she passed through the doorway, to see Carrie's body still lying on the floor next to Mark's.

She turned and walked back in, and sat down in front of the monitor. She reached out as if to touch the image of Carrie. To no avail, she can't touch her. She lowered her hand and sat back in the chair.

I came up behind Sam and placed my hands on her shoulders. Trying to comfort someone on a day like this seemed impossible.

"Mike, what did she say to you?"

Still looking at the screen I started to tell her. "She wants me to trust her and she will get us out."

"Call her; ask her to come in here please."

I didn't know how this worked, so I just called out Carrie's name. She was our sensitive and this was her gig. I called out her name again and asked her to come into the parlor with us.

Sam kept staring at the monitor and I looked down too. The figure on the second floor started to move towards the stairway. Though we saw her legs move, the motion was different and she flowed down the hall. Sam rushed to the door as to greet a friend that hasn't been seen in years. But no one came in, that we could see at least.

Samantha body drooped in disappointment and she turn towards me. She held back the tears and walked towards my open arms. I held her tight and reassured her that we would be ok. I didn't believe it but I had to say it.

"Carrie, are you here? Can you do something to show us you're in the room?"

The lights flickered on and off, not even a second after I asked. I let go of Sam and sat on the couch. I closed my eyes like I saw Carrie do a hundred times and called out to her.

"Carrie how are we going to get out?"

"Mike, I will clear a way for you to the back door. Mrs. Chatterley will try to stop you and have you join us here. It is Elizabeth; she is seeking revenge on everyone who enters this house. When she fell to her death she cursed Charles and this house. She felt like he ripped her heart out so she wants to do that to that to everyone who walks through the door."

"Charles is here." continued Carrie's voice. "He will help you out also. His sorrow is great and she is keeping his spirit here. To walk these halls in misery for eternity."

"Now Mike when its time you and Samantha need to run. Run as fast as you can. Do not stop! Do not try to open the door just put your shoulder to it and run!"

"Carrie." I muttered, "I am sorry. I never meant for this to happen to you and Mark."

"I know, and we are ok. Now we need to save you and Sam."

This gave me a little consult but not enough. I don't ever think that I will ever forgive myself, nor get over this experience.

"Mike when you hear the door slam, grab Samantha and run to the door. Don't stop, please Mike don't stop till you're outside!"

I nodded my head and agreed. I looked at Sam and told her that I knew what to do.

15

I got up and walked to Sam. My heart was pounding so hard I thought she would be able to see it through my shirt. I tried to keep my nerve so Sam would be calm. I reached out and held her hand and gave a halfhearted smile.

"It's almost time." I said to Samantha, still hoping it would work.

We stood there for what seemed to be an eternity. Just looking into each other's eyes, at this point I could tell how much I loved her. The moment was interrupted by a loud bang. I turned and looked at the monitor and the door going outside was closed.

"We need to run!" I said to Sam as I started to run out of the room. Pulling her arm almost out of the socket I dragged her behind me.

I noticed Mark and Carrie's bodies were gone. The broken rail was mended, like it never happened. We ran through the foyer and everything happened so fast.

Lights began to flicker, and the house started to look like it was breathing. Walls expanded and contracted, pictures on the wall fell. Crashing sounds were all around us.

As we entered the dining room chairs moved away from the table and started to fly towards us. The chandelier swung around in circles over our heads. We bypassed all of that without being hit by a chair or any other flying debris.

We continued into the kitchen and ran along the counter. Cabinet doors opened as well as drawer. It was like the drawers were pulled out such a fashion to have its contents fly out. Dishes and glasses flying around, breaking around us on the floor as we ran past.

The bad thing is a figure appeared in front of the door. It was Elizabeth, she was blocking our way. I was told not to stop; I have to go through her. Right then a cold wind went past my head, not once but twice.

I watched as to bright lights flew towards Mrs. Chatterley and it looked like it engulfed her and lifted her out of the way. I let go of Sam's hand and lowered my shoulder. I hit the door at full speed and it flew open.

I sped through the door falling as I got outside. As I hit the ground I looked back to see Sam exiting the house right behind me and fall as I have done.

Ghost Hunted

The door slammed behind us and that banshee scream filled our ears once again.

15

We lay upon on the ground trying to catch our breath. Taking in fresh air and I noticed that the sun was coming up. This was the most beautiful sun rise I have ever seen.

As I rolled to my side I saw Samantha was breathing hard. She glanced over and for the first time in hours I saw a smile appear on her face. I crawled over to her and kissed her. I kissed her hard letting my tongue touch hers.

As I pulled away from her I told her I loved her and wanted to never be without her. I would ask her to marry me but the timing wasn't right. We lost our friends and

I was thinking of popping the question. Smooth move on my part.

I got to my feet and helped Sam off the ground. She brushed loose grass off her pants, like that would help her appearance any. Shit we just went through hell, and as she looked up she still looked perfect to me. Beyond the dirt and grime, she was still beautiful.

We cautiously started to walk around the side of the house. It was eerily quiet, considering what happened. As we got close to the front of the house we heard a moan. And it was outside; I was thinking nothing could get out of the house.

We got closer to the sound and noticed it was coming from a bush. Next to the bush was a dirty shoe, with dog crap on it. It was Kevin, and he was lying in the bush.

He had cuts over his face and arm. But he was alive and kicking, well not kicking he was swearing.

"Kev are you ok?" I asked him.

"I think my leg is broke. And I have blood running down my arm."

"Sam help me get him out of there!" I said as I reached down to him. Since he was thrown out the window he survived the night.

We stood him up and wrapped our arms around him and helped him to the van. He sat on the edge of the running board and we told him what happened as we checked on his leg. Sam cleaned up his leg and confirmed his leg was broken.

When I finished telling him what happened, he started crying and looked up at me in disbelief. I told him everything was true and that our three friends were still lying in the house dead.

We sat there for a moment and looked back to the house. It looked the same as it did when we got there the night before. Nothing changed, not even the window

Kevin fell through. There wasn't even a crack.

Sam and I helped Kevin all the way into the van and Sam plugged her phone into the car charger. She got into the van and closed the door. She slouched back in the seat with total exhaustion.

I walked around to the driver's side to get in, but I had to look back one more time. On the porch I saw my friend, Carrie. She stood there to see us off.

"Rest well my friend, be peaceful." I said to her.

"Mike you will see me again. I will be around you always…..trust me."

With a tear in my eye I smiled and continued to the door and climbed in.

16

We took Kevin to the hospital and waited there until his mother got there. At that time we said good bye to Kevin and left for home.

The ride back to the house was long and quiet. Sam looked like she was about ready to pass out. I myself was still in shock with what happened. I pulled into the driveway and we exited the van.

I opened the van door and helped Samantha out, then led her up the stairs holding her hand. As the knob turned I pushed the door open and let her in as I followed.

She kicked off her shoes and padded her way to the kitchen. I tossed my keys on the coffee table and followed her. She leaned against the counter and covered her face. I knew she couldn't cry anymore. It was over and we both needed to accept it.

"Never again Mike, never again!"

I agreed and passed her to make some coffee. She said we should call the police and tell them. She picked up the phone and I listened to what she said. I could hear the laughing from the other end but they said they would check it out.

I looked in the refrigerator and pulled out some eggs. I offered to make breakfast and she accepted. I grabbed some more things out of the fridge and placed them on the counter.

"I need to take a shower and call in to work. I just can't make it today." She said in a soft voice.

"I will have food ready when you get back down babe."

As she left the room I poured myself a cup of coffee and started to cook some eggs and hash browns. I walked up stairs to bring a cup of coffee to Sam; she was taking her clothes off in the bedroom.

Dirt lines were definite where her clothes ended. As she took off her bra I asked her if she wanted a drink. She said yes and turned towards me. The bad thing is I felt a little turned on.

I sat on the bed watching her sip her coffee topless. She set the cup down on the dresser and proceeded to pull off her underwear. I gave her a smile and she looked back at me in disgust.

"Really?"

That was all she said as she went out the room and walked into the bathroom shutting and locking the door behind her. Well, end of that.

And we finally found out who killed Mr. Chatterley. It was Elizabeth Chatterley, she also killed my friends. She was a pure evil spirit, fueling on anger and revenge. I am deeply sorry for what happened. All there is to do now is wait for the police.

As I headed back down to the kitchen I heard the shower start. I hit the edge of the stairs and I heard Sam scream. I ran back yelling at the door and no response back. I kicked the door in and pulled back the shower curtain.

Sam was lying at the bottom of the tub with a hole in her chest. I looked up and Elizabeth Chatterley appeared in front of me. With the banshee yell she came flying towards me pushing me through the doorway into the bedroom across the hall.

My feet were not even touching the ground. And she kept pushing me through the small room and out the window. I fell the two stories and hit the ground with a thud. As I hit I felt my right arm snap and my head hit a rock. I looked up to see Elizabeth standing at the window laughing.

She killed my friends and my lover and she stood there laughing. Then she disappeared while the sound of her laughing echoed through my head. Everything went black while the sounds of sirens filled the street.

Things going on around me seemed distant and my mind wandered as I remembered my friends. My love is gone, now I wonder if life is worth living. That will be something I need to find out.

About the author

Jason was born and raised in a suburb outside of Chicago. Living mainly with his father and grandmother after the age of ten, he was a normal kid. Not that great of a student he made his way through high school and finally graduated.

He tried living the rock and roll life style into his mid-twenties then decided to go back to school. At that time he decided to go to a trade school instead of college. A counselor told him he had a form of dyslexia and it could be the biggest reason he did poorly. Throughout school he did rather well, scoring in the top five percent of his class.

But that did not last long. He felt he was learning more in his trade working then at the school. So he dropped out and pursued his work. Many hits and misses came through his life but he battled through.

At the age of twenty seven he lost his best friend, his father. He felt alone and lost. Within the next three years he got married and had two beautiful daughters.

The marriage didn't last and he was on his own again. After learning how to drive a truck he felt like his life finally started to look up. Then another blow to him, a back injury changed his life.

Not being able to drive a truck anymore he elected to go through back surgery. As he was being put under, Jason stopped breathing, finding out later that he was allergic to penicillin. After Jason found out the surgery was a bust and that he nearly died he decided to change his life.

Although he believes in the paranormal he did not think he had any near death experience. But his interest heightened, and after meeting his present wife the both started investigating.

Now living in Moline, IL and married Jason still wanted to improve himself. He started writing. Mostly he writes about the paranormal, taking some experiences and cases and making into a fiction story.

With dyslexia still in his path he works forth and battles against the odds.

Ghost Hunted

Ghost Hunted

Ghost Hunted

www.ingramcontent.com/pod-product-compliance
Lightning Source LLC
Chambersburg PA
CBHW052054070526
44584CB00017B/2173